First published 2009 by Walker Books Ltd
87 Vauxhall Walk, London SE11 5HJ

2 4 6 8 10 9 7 5 3 1

Printed and bound in Italy by ☙ Grafica Veneta S.p.A.

British Library Cataloguing in Publication Data:
a catalogue record for this book is available from the British Library

ISBN 978-1-4063-2048-0

www.walker.co.uk

www.andiwatson.biz

for Philippa

None of them any help to Glister.

...really, Miss Butterworth, the day is closing, and I'd like to finish this chapter.

But what do you **REALLY** want?

To finish the chapter this evening.

Sigh.

Then Glister began to feel strange. Her vision wavered and blurred like she was seeing the world through sepia jelly.

Philippa Veil

Philippa took up residence in one of Chilblain Hall's many spare rooms.

A DAY IN THE AFTERLIFE OF Philippa Veil

The afterlife of a novelist can be just as fretful as their first life. With Albert Buckle sitting smug and completed on a shelf, Philippa Veil's other unfinished works come back to haunt her.

Today I shall not think of writing but sit and enjoy a nice cup of tea. After which, perhaps a trip to the shops.

Work on me.

No, me.

Me, me, me!

Who are you again?

That, madam, is the problem. I am your Gothic Novel. A book still awaiting a title.

Centuries without so much as a name to my name. Do you realize, madam, the humiliation I suffer at the hands of your younger works?

Nobby-no-name.

Untitled and unloved.

I'm not listening – I refuse to write today. Perhaps tomorrow.

WHAT Mr Wilkes DID NEXT?

Mr Wilkes had learned nothing from his haunted teapot experience. Only a week or so later a strange figure appeared on his doorstep...

The unfortunate fellow had the bad luck to get on the wrong side of Queen Liz, by standing on her toes during her favourite Quadrille.

Bish-bosh, next thing I know I'm in the Tower. A nasty business with an axe followed, and I've been searching for the old bonce ever since.

I think it might be your lucky day, my friend.

Oh, good show!

What's that you're doing?

Glister · THE HOUSE HUNT

When word of the Bonny Village Competition (TM) reaches Gravehunger Moss, Mr Swarkstone heads the local task force.

Leonard Swarkstone, Lord Lieutenant of Whixleyshire. Terribly efficient but of a tidy mind.

He's determined to bring the trophy and the glory home to the village. Only one thing stands in his way...

CHILBLAIN HALL.

Mr Swarkstone wasn't very enthusiastic about Chilblain's eccentric charms.

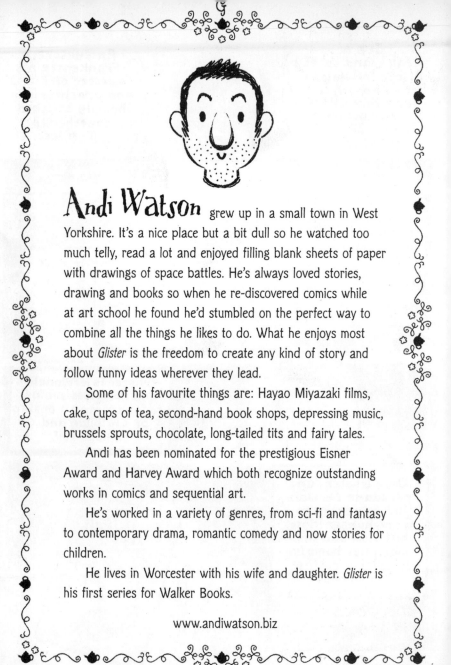

Andi Watson grew up in a small town in West Yorkshire. It's a nice place but a bit dull so he watched too much telly, read a lot and enjoyed filling blank sheets of paper with drawings of space battles. He's always loved stories, drawing and books so when he re-discovered comics while at art school he found he'd stumbled on the perfect way to combine all the things he likes to do. What he enjoys most about *Glister* is the freedom to create any kind of story and follow funny ideas wherever they lead.

Some of his favourite things are: Hayao Miyazaki films, cake, cups of tea, second-hand book shops, depressing music, brussels sprouts, chocolate, long-tailed tits and fairy tales.

Andi has been nominated for the prestigious Eisner Award and Harvey Award which both recognize outstanding works in comics and sequential art.

He's worked in a variety of genres, from sci-fi and fantasy to contemporary drama, romantic comedy and now stories for children.

He lives in Worcester with his wife and daughter. *Glister* is his first series for Walker Books.

www.andiwatson.biz